POTENTIAL GRIZZLIES

POTENTIAL GRIZZLIES

Making the Nonsense Bearable

Kevin G. Welner

INFORMATION AGE PUBLISHING, INC.
Charlotte, NC • www.infoagepub.com

Library of Congress Cataloging-in-Publication Data

A CIP record for this book is available from the Library of Congress
http://www.loc.gov

ISBN: 978-1-64802-297-5 (Paperback)
978-1-64802-298-2 (Hardcover)
978-1-64802-299-9 (E-Book)

Cover: Grizzly bear photo from Adam Van Spronsen/Shutterstock. DeVos shooting
photo uses headshot from Gage Skidmore, as well as a woman with an assault rifle,
photo from UfaBizPhoto/Shutterstock

CONTENTS

FOREWORD

It's difficult for first-rate scholars to come face to face with absurd claims, programs, and suggestions by those they consider pompous, ignorant, misguided, or lying. It's harder still to respond in respectful, "proper" ways. But scholars can nonetheless feel straightjacketed and bound to keep up pretenses.

Of course, many disagreements about research, the nature of "facts," and the analyses of policy must be met with seriousness. But some such disagreements are better met with a response that is humorous—playful, ironic, sarcastic. This is especially true when confronting an interpretation of facts or policies that's obviously the result of someone's highly idiosyncratic personal experiences, politics, or immutable intransigence—or simply a display of ignorance.

It is when serious argument—*the cornerstone of good social science*—disappears that humorous responses are most appropriate. Silliness and absurdity, and their cousin, ridicule, are proper responses to inadequate research in support of a political ideology, and of just plain hare-brained ideas! Monty Python's Flying Circus was a hit show in multiple nations, but this was not because the troupe *seriously* dealt with a broad array of important family, social, and political issues. It was a hit because absurdity became the appropriate response to the corresponding absurdity of the purportedly serious debate presented by their nations' government and social leaders.

Thank goodness scholars like Kevin Welner recognize that. To be playful in a world of seriousness is to give most of us a well needed break, a smile, and even a hearty laugh. Welner finds a way to amusingly challenge (or dismiss) people, research, and arguments that really should not ever have been given much credence. So, enjoy this wry medley of Welner's humor. Smile and maybe laugh out loud, as he, and we all, deal with the quite serious issues of public education in a contentious, often discordant democracy—frequently led by silly people!

—**David C. Berliner**
Regents' Professor Emeritus
Arizona State University
Tempe, AZ

ACKNOWLEDGMENTS

This book arose outside of my scholarly work, with no purpose other than the entertainment of myself and a few friends and colleagues. I doubt I would have bothered writing even a second or third "Ed Tweak" without the encouragement and suggestions from those wacky kids Gene Glass, Ken Howe, Martin Lipton, and David Berliner. As I recall, the "Operate for America" idea came from Martin. Ken, according to well-founded rumor, apparently shared one of the *Ed Tweak* publications during his presentation of my case for promotion to full professor. It takes a special friend to know that a promotion-deliberation was just the time I wanted this work to be shared with my most senior colleagues.

Beyond that cheering section, my foremost thanks go to my friend of 40 years, Don Weitzman, who gave a first read to so many of the pieces now included in this book, providing creative suggestions along the way.

Finally, thank you to my family for encouraging me to take this risk. Scholars, once we've established ourselves in our niches, have a bit of a safe zone within which we can largely coast along. We don't need to take chances, let alone the book-writer's version of hesitantly climbing onto stage for open mic night at a comedy club. But what the heck. With COVID-19 parked over our collective heads and face-to-face human interaction a thing of the past, I can risk the cyber-mortification. Thanks, Lena!

INTRODUCTION

A dozen years ago, following the birth of my daughter, I was fortunate to be able to take a semester-long paid parental leave to stay home with her. Almost every day she'd fall asleep while attached to me in a baby carrier. So I'd find myself sitting down to rest, often in front of the computer, while she contentedly snoozed on my chest. Since I had little inclination to do actual work, I started writing up *Onion*-inspired "news" stories to share with friends.

This continued, with varying degrees of dedication and productivity, over the following decade.[1] I usually formatted the pieces as a publication with the title, "*Education Tweak*." That name was a bit of a misnomer, since the satire wasn't directed at *Ed Week* but rather at *Education Next*, the pro-market-reform magazine connected to the Hoover Institute, the Fordham Institute, and the Harvard Kennedy School Program on Education Policy and Governance. I loosely modeled the visuals after *Education Next*, and many of those early pieces were inspired by the articles it published that breathlessly touted the benefits of school choice, teacher merit pay, and test-based accountability reform. Over the years, the scope of my topics expanded, and my venue would sometimes shift from *Ed Tweak* to the annual April Fools newsletters of the National Education Policy Center (NEPC), which I direct.

I was initially motivated to start writing April Fools newsletters back in 2015 when opponents of NEPC attacked our pro-public-education work as a cynical ploy to garner funding from the two national teachers unions. The irony was that NEPC has always run on a shoestring budget, while so-called reform organizations had budgets and staffing levels far larger. So we sent off this newsletter:[2]

NEPC EMBRACES NEW REFORMY MISSION

BOULDER, CO (April 1, 2015)—The National Education Policy Center today announced that it is changing its mission statement and renouncing the pursuit of strong, equitable public schools.

NEPC director Kevin Welner admitted that the whole enterprise had been a ruse, and that he and his colleagues were really only in it for the money and for the elation of constant policy victories.

The NEPC's mission statement in support of that ruse has been "to produce and disseminate high-quality, peer-reviewed research to inform education policy discussions . . . guided by the belief that the democratic governance of public education is strengthened when policies are based on sound evidence."

Welner announced that the new mission statement would be "to promote policies that have a surface appeal, that are built on the whimsical magic of the free market, and that use schools to facilitate the reproduction of inequalities from generation to generation." Research evidence, Welner added, would be generated whenever necessary to prop up these goals.

"We know that by abandoning our past mission we'll have to forgo the immense funding advantages that come from caring about high-quality evidence, equity, and public schooling. But that was never really us. There comes a time when we must set aside our crass pursuit of financial gain and dedicate ourselves to our true ideals. If this means trying to squeeze money from financially strapped hedge fund managers or 're-form-focused' foundations with tiny endowments, then that's just what we will have to do," said Welner.

Not everyone understood the humor (or noticed the calendar date). I recall the NEPC email account receiving a couple angry messages from followers who felt betrayed.

During the Obama presidency, my writing frequently targeted Secretary of Education Arne Duncan for his non-evidence-based agenda that intensified the Bush administration's testing and accountability policies. For example, there was this short item:

DUNCAN FINDS SHORTCUT IN PREPARATION FOR SENATE HEARINGS

Advisors preparing Education Secretary designate Arne Duncan for his Senate confirmation hearings have made the fortuitous discovery that they are able to use the same talking points used by Bush education secretaries Margaret Spellings and Rod Paige. "All we had to do was take out the part about vouchers and tone down some of the stuff about how awful public schools are. Arne's pretty comfortable with the rest," said an advisor who requested confidentiality.

Then, soon after the Obama State of the Union address where Rep. Joe Wilson shouted "You lie!" in response to an Obama statement about his health-care-reform proposal, I wrote this piece:

SEC'TY DUNCAN'S OUTBURSTS MAR RESEARCH CONFERENCE

This year's annual conference about research on education was repeatedly interrupted by cries of "You lie!" by U.S. Secretary of Education Arne Duncan.

The initial incident occurred on Tuesday morning during a session about charter schools. Members of the audience reported that Duncan, who was sitting near the front, jumped to his feet and shouted, "You lie!" just after a panelist said, "We now know beyond any reasonable doubt that charter schools are not likely to drive substantial innovation or improvements in student achievement."

Later, during a Tuesday afternoon session about alternative approaches to principal and teacher evaluation and compensation, the Secretary again leapt up, yelling, "You lie! You lie!" when a panelist explained that tests should be used only for the purpose for which they were developed and that "tests developed to assess student knowledge have not been validated for use in evaluating teachers or principals."

Five minutes later, when the same panelist said that research on test-score-based teacher evaluation is under-developed and could not support a major scaling up of the policy, Duncan could be heard throughout the auditorium repeating "You lie!

You liar! You lie!"

When asked about these outbursts, the Secretary insisted that they were all justified. "I've done a magnificent job surrounding myself with people who pretend that the research actually supports our policies. So it's just wrong for me to have to hear anything contradicting that. Rest assured, I'll have a stern talk with my scheduler when I get back to the office."

Another piece critiqued the Department of Education's funding priorities:

U.S. DEPARTMENT OF EDUCATION AWARDS $3 MILLION TO BOB

During a news conference at the Department of Education yesterday, Bob gave repeated thanks to U.S. taxpayers for their generosity. Holding up an oversized novelty check for his $3 million grant, Bob acknowledged the economic downturn that has put a financial squeeze on ordinary Americans, "At a time when most of my fellow citizens are struggling, I can't help but be amazed by how magnanimous [Education Secretary] Arne Duncan is with their money."

Bob's grant will hand out the latest of tens of millions of dollars that the U.S. Department of Education has given to Duncan's friends and allies. Asked how he ended up as the newest beneficiary, Bob told reporters about how Duncan started chatting with him at an IHOP just outside Kalamazoo. "At first I thought it was strange, this guy just out of the blue asking if I had any thoughts about the school system, but he seemed like a nice fellow."

"So I says to him, 'We need to make schools more modern. No more of this old stuff. We've gotta break down union resistance. They're always against change and protecting the status quo and all like that. And we should assign numbers and grades to teachers. Numbers don't lie. And parents should have lots of choices. It doesn't matter what they're choosing, but they need a whole lot of those choices.' I showed Mr. Duncan all the syrups we could get for our pancakes and asked how he'd feel if he only had blueberry syrup. And I could see that he really understood my point. So then I told him that we should finally hold schools and educrats accountable. Oh, and how come we don't unleash the awesome power of competition and the free market? We've gotta do that, too. Cut through lots of red tape. And technology, I really like technology. But what I'm really all about is new ideas that inspire!"

"So I'm talking, and Mr. Duncan takes out his iPad and jots down all sorts of notes. He's nodding and smiling and then when I'm finished he says, 'You're a reformer, young man. And I want to give you $3 million dollars.' I thought he was kidding at first, but I looked it up. He does this all the time. There are charter school corporations like KIPP, Rocketship, Uncommon Schools, IDEA, and Harmony. And there are groups like Teach for America and TNTP. So why not me?"

"We were truly moved by Bob's unique brand of innovation, just like his chocolate chip pancakes. We are looking forward to Bob bringing his vision to classrooms across the country," said Secretary Duncan in making the award announcement.

During the administration of George W. Bush, I speculated about how Education Secretary Margaret Spellings might confront the problem of what to do if No Child Left Behind's 6-year sequence of escalating consequences were insufficient. What happens the subsequent year?

The current version of NCLB requires that a school failing to make AYP [Adequate Yearly Progress] for 6 years must restructure, with four specific options identified: replacing the principal and the entire staff, reopening as a charter school, contracting with a private school management company, or a state takeover of the school from the district.

The proposal for reauthorization looks to the year after that deadline, requiring that the teachers and students of a school failing to make AYP for 7 consecutive years be subjected to "alternative motivation techniques" (AMTs).

At Tuesday's press conference, Spellings acknowledged that the pre- ferred AMT, and at this point the only one that would be approved by her department, was waterboarding . . .

Soon after this, we found ourselves in the era of school leaders and policymakers attacking teacher unions, so I wrote the following Jodie Foster inspired piece:

GOV. WALKER SAYS HE DID IT
TO IMPRESS MICHELLE RHEE

Wisconsin Governor Scott Walker yesterday admitted that his union-busting agenda was just his way of trying to impress Michelle Rhee, the former DC schools chancellor.

Walker says he first became entranced by Rhee when he saw a video clip of her talking about taping shut the mouths of her students. Then, when he watched *Waiting for Superman*, he realized they were eternally connected. "When I heard her bashing unions, I knew she was talking to me, like we were on our own private wavelength, and I knew what she meant for me to do. She was telling me to break the backs of the unions to earn her love. I couldn't fight it."

According to Walker, he started laying out his plan the very next day. "People think it was the Koch brothers and their billions, but it wasn't. I was driven by my muse. I could have never found the strength, were it not for Michelle."

But things haven't gone as Walker had hoped. For one thing,

Rhee started hanging out with other besotted Republican governors, Chris Christie of New Jersey and Rick Scott of Florida, both of whom wooed her with promises of massive privatizing of public education.

Walker was unsure if Rhee was just playing coy or if she had forsaken him because he was unworthy of her love. But a new opportunity presented itself when he learned that Rhee routinely gave awards to schools that cheated to improve their test scores. "She clearly likes bad boys," he realized. So, as an act of sheer desperation, he decided to flagrantly violate the Wisconsin open meetings law.

Alas, even this offering has failed to catch Rhee's eye. Most days now, Governor Walker sits alone, staring sadly at the life-sized posters of Rhee that adorn his office and wondering what he did wrong. He's sure, though, that it's unionized teachers' fault. "Someday a real rain will come and wash all this scum out of the classrooms," he said between muffled sobs.

The pieces that follow are more evergreen than these examples—less tied to a specific news event. But before turning to those "Ed Tweaks," I will offer up one more topical piece. It was based on the right-wing uproar prior to President Obama's September 8, 2009 back-to-school speech that was broadcast to students during the school day. The banal message of the actual speech was just "work hard," but the fears expressed were of socialist indoctrination or worse. I wrote the following:

OBAMA USES BLACK MAGIC
IN SPEECH TO INNOCENTS

Seizing on his unprecedented access to impressionable youth, President Obama used today's speech, shown in classrooms throughout the nation, to compel America's white children to become black. Obama summoned his hypnotic voodoo powers to convince the children to "break away from the shackles of whiteness" and join his revolution.

The president took advantage of the underdeveloped capacity for resistance of his young audience, overwhelming them through the force of his magnetic, Svengali-like charm. "The dusky peoples of the earth are the future," he said with a warm smile and kind voice. "Once you've gone black there ain't no coming back." He added "Join us, or you will be conquered."

Local Schools Superintendent Bernie Boote has been getting angry calls from parents, but he defended his decision to allow the broadcast in the district's classrooms. "He was supposed to talk about staying in school and working hard. It was supposed to be pabulum. The text I was sent said inane things like, 'that's no excuse for neglecting your homework or having a bad attitude. That's no excuse for talking back to your teacher.' It was supposed to be harmless, silly nonsense like that, that the kids would laugh at. He wasn't supposed to get into that race war thing."

But school board member Katie Cross disagreed and pointed out that the speech had been prophesized. "This is exactly what Glenn Beck's been warning us about. Boote refused to listen. He just refused to listen…"

"We're worried," said parent Karen Smith. "It's not just that our little Madison wants to turn black. If all her schoolmates do it too, who will Madison date? Even if she becomes black, we still wouldn't want her to date one of them."

That was one of the edgier pieces I wrote, made more so by the accompanying photo of the president shaking hands with a young Black teenager, with the photo description reading, "Just 5 minutes earlier, little Mickey O'Shaunnessy was a freckled, tousle-haired White boy."

For me, writing the *Ed Tweaks* served as a way to blow off steam, and my small cohort of appreciative readers convinced me to keep at it. Eventually, I wrote 75 or so stories, the majority of which (the "evergreen" ones) are included in this book. They're presented in topical groupings; school choice stories in one group, test-based accountability stories in another, etc. I also include a brief rundown at the outset of each issue, to provide the minimal background for readers who shamefully neglected to keep completely abreast of education policy over the past dozen years.

If you find any of the following to be offensive or unpleasing in any way, please do not hesitate to send your thoughts to Betsy.DeVos@ed.gov.

Notes

1. The "Ungifted to Use Fewer Resources" story is derived from a piece I co-authored even earlier: Welner, K. G., & Welner, K. M. (1999). *Giftwrapping inequality*. National Council of Advocates for Students.
2. This newsletter has a couple small wording changes from the original, as do others presented in this book.

THE USE OF RESEARCH (OR NOT) BY POLICYMAKERS

O ne of my recurrent themes is the failure of policymakers to acknowledge, or quite possibly to read, the research on the policies they're making. I'm reminded of an incident years ago, when a policymaker met with a group of doctoral students and faculty in my program at the University of Colorado Boulder. He touted a policy approach that we knew had a poor track record. One of the doctoral students politely asked something to the effect, "The research on X is disappointing. Does that give you any pause?" His response: "Research can be made to say anything." (That policymaker has since risen to an even more powerful elected office.)

An impressive body of research may counsel in favor of smaller class sizes or high-quality early-childhood education or intensive early intervention programs in math and reading. Or it may counsel against grade retention or academic tracking. No matter. Policymaking continues along its own path, undeterred by evidence. Researchers must accept some of the blame, when we fail to communicate our work beyond small academic circles. But the larger policymaking system is also broken. This theme will occasionally re-emerge in other articles later in this book, but the first item below is the only place where I addressed it directly.

Potential Grizzlies, pages 1–5
Copyright © 2021 by Information Age Publishing
All rights of reproduction in any form reserved.

The second item below takes on a related issue, which is the narrow understanding of high-quality research. Some policymakers and even some researchers elevate so-called randomized controlled trials (RCTs) as the "gold standard," meaning that results from such studies are more trustworthy than other research results—or even that RCTs are the only studies that should be heeded. These research designs do have the potential to yield results that make strong causal inferences, but they also have important limitations—something that the second piece below has a bit of fun with.

CONNECTION DISCOVERED BETWEEN RESEARCH AND POLICY

A team of scientists from leading universities announced yesterday that they have discovered the long-hypothesized connection between educational research and policy. Using an electron microscope, the scientists found filamentary threads of evidence linking the two.

The discovery generated particular excitement among scholars of education, who had long ago accepted their own complete inconsequentialness in any practical sense. "The underlying premise of discourse in our milieu has been obscurity," said leading scholar Dr. Paul Miro. "Perchance, as per this evidence, I shall forthwith scriven using lucid verbiage."

For years, historians had speculated that the elusive research-policy connection would emerge every few decades, only to then quickly fade. Known as the "ephemeral link" hypothesis, this speculation fell into disfavor during the NCLB period, for obvious reasons. Today's announcement, however, will doubtless re-energize the field, with archeologists

Team leader, Stanford Professor Paul Gannow, looking thrilled about his discovery.

already said to be planning expeditions.

Others were less enthused. Contacted for comment, a leading educational policymaker called the scientists' claims "nonsense." Speaking on condition of anonymity, she explained, "We're impervious to empirical evidence, and no so-called research will ever change my opinion on that."

GOLD-STANDARD RESEARCH FOUND
TO CONSIST OF FOOL'S GOLD

A startling discovery made last week in a Chicago laboratory is poised to turn the educational research world on its head. Randomized controlled trials (RCTs), long thought to be the gold standard for research, were found to consist almost entirely of iron pyrite, popularly known as "fool's gold."

In the realm of the hard sciences, most notably in pharmaceutical testing, experimental designs such as double-blind studies using a placebo are indeed atomic-number-79 and thus real gold. Educational researchers naturally assumed that experimental designs were equally ideal for their work.

Yet when the Chicago researchers carefully inspected RCTs, they discerned few of the benefits of true experimental studies. "The subjects ordinarily weren't blind to whether they were in the treatment or control group, there was almost always no placebo, the subjects usually were not representative of the general population, and neither the treatment nor control subjects would stay in their proper place," explained Dr. Fess Au, the lead investigator of the Chicago scientists who made the discovery.

Au notes that the research team did find some RCT specimens, such as those investigating a well-defined curricular intervention, that merited more attention. But the majority of RCTs clearly had little gold content.

To illustrate, Au pointed to studies of charter schools. Because some charter schools are popular and then use a lottery to determine who will be offered admission, researchers can take advantage of that random assignment of applicants to each of the two groups: those offered admission and those denied admission. Au pointed to five problems:

1. Those offered admission sometimes don't accept.
2. Those denied admission sometimes find a comparable treatment (a similar school), so the idea of a "control" group becomes murky.
3. Those who start at the charter school sometimes leave, and the researchers often don't know why.
4. Because any given charter school provides different instructional approaches and resources, "charter school reform" isn't a well-defined intervention.
5. Both groups of subjects know their status (treatment or control), potentially generating a Hawthorne effect, whereby they differentially change their behavior.
6. Even assuming all the other problems are addressed, the results cannot be generalized beyond the specific context and types of subjects.

"It's this last point that really made us realize we were looking at fool's gold," said Au. "How much does it help us to know that a particular, over-enrolled charter school has X effect on Y students?" He explained that the results cannot be generalized to other charter schools, and certainly not to less popular charter schools. The results also cannot be generalized to the broad population of "non-chooser" families that did not apply to the school (or to any charter school).

"The usual result," the scientists concluded, "is good internal validity but weak external validity. So why all the fuss?"

Seeking to answer this question, we tracked down three researchers known for their RCT work. All three spoke only on condition of anonymity, and all acknowledged the scarcity of true gold in their work. "The real gold in this research comes from the

IES," said one, referring to the federal Institute of Education Sciences, which awards over $100 million in grants

Glitter.

every year and strongly favors RCT research.

REFORMINESS

The next four articles introduce us to the word that has dominated education policy for decades: *reform*. Through a lavishly funded and triumphant effort, "reform" in education has broken free of its dictionary shackles, where its meaning has long been confined to signifying "change" or "improvement." To qualify now as a reform in education, that change must be in the direction approved by the reformy overlords. In fact, improvement on the current system does not generally make the cut as real reform. Only disruption or replacement of public schools, or their teachers, will do.

The first two articles below address reform in a general sense, so the only additional point I'll make here concerns the discussion of "growth models" in the second article. These are statistical approaches that attempt to isolate the contribution—the likely effect—of a given input (e.g., a particular teacher or school) to a given output (e.g., the test score growth of that teacher's or school's students). Accountability systems based on students' test scores were originally focused, under the "No Child Left Behind" regime, on increasing the number of students who scored at or above proficiency on high-stakes tests. Newer accountability systems that use growth models rely on those same test scores but instead ask whether these students' scores are increasing at the requisite pace.

Following those two articles, I address a particular reform idea: The Broad Academy. The academy was created to provide an alternative way of

Potential Grizzlies, pages 7–12
Copyright © 2021 by Information Age Publishing
7

preparing leaders of urban school districts, and it has been enormously successful in placing its graduates in superintendencies (in, e.g., Los Angeles, Chicago, Philadelphia, Oklahoma City, Detroit, Oakland, and Denver) as well as top state positions (in, e.g., New Jersey and Rhode Island). The academy's graduates generally bring to their new jobs a resplendently reformy agenda, aligned with the advocacy of billionaire Eli Broad, the academy's founder and benefactor. The third story below was inspired by the pattern of school districts hiring business leaders as superintendents, partly represented by the Broad Academy and partly a broader (ahem) trend.

The fourth and final article in this section concerns "Democrats for Education Reform" (DfER), an advocacy group that encourages Democrats to support the version of school reform described above. In particular, DfER strongly supports the growth of the charter school sector, especially so-called "charter management organizations" (networks of charter schools run by a centralized corporate office), as well as the high-stakes evaluation of teachers based on the growth scores of their students. Many of the characters who show up throughout this book are associated with DfER, including former Secretary of Education Arne Duncan.

PRESTIGIOUS TASK FORCE CALLS ON
REFORMERS TO REDOUBLE THEIR FAILURES

The Elm Institute's Commission on Educational Castigation returned from their retreat at a five-star hotel in Monte Carlo to launch a campaign for more fiscal restraint and stronger accountability measures.

"The complete failure of these reform measures over the last forty years shows that we simply have not been trying hard enough. We must double down on our failures," reads the Commission's declaration.

Learning from those failures, the Commission now points to the need to make it absolutely clear to schools that they must do more with less. "Sometimes it seems like teachers want taxpayers to provide both the chalkboard *and* the chalk," said Commission Chair

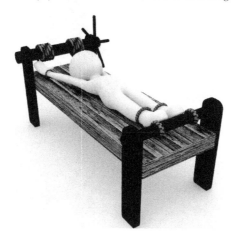

Consequences.

Tiffany Prescott. "There's no pleasing these people. More to the point, why should we coddle when we are perfectly able to impose consequences? Teachers do better, and children learn more, when they are intensely afraid that hellfire will rain down on them if they come up short."

Before boarding her corporate jet, Prescott also said that schools can learn a great deal from the private business sector. She explained, "Simply put, our study panel focused with laser-like intensity on creating an inclusive, deep restructuring design to meet the increasing demands of the 21st century workforce based on non-governmental synergy among partners and stakeholders to leverage multiplicative forces for exponential rewards."

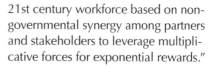

GROWTH MODELS RECOGNIZED FOR AVOIDING RECOGNITION OF POLICY FAILURE

Former Education Secretaries Arne Duncan and Margaret Spellings today jointly bestowed growth models with a special recognition for their key role in preventing policymakers and others from recognizing the failure of high-stakes, test-based accountability policies.

Secretary Spellings explained that the shift from "adequate yearly progress" goals to growth goals represented a corresponding and historic shift. "This moves us away from demanding that test scores of all children be above an arbitrary annual threshold and toward demanding that those test scores improve by an arbitrary amount each year." Growth modeling, she explained, offers a solution to the problem of having to do something to address the fundamental failure of the NCLB approach.

Nope, no policy failures down here.

Secretary Duncan explained that the change in the nation's education policy was monumental, allowing observers to see a new policy that looks very different, at first glance. He promised that the new policy would "significantly slow the rate" of the increase in education gaps.

Spellings and Duncan both embraced the idea that all children who are left behind should raise their test scores by three percent per year until such a time as they graduate or retire. "Kids might need books, qualified teachers, healthy facilities, and medical care," said Spellings, "but that's no excuse for them to believe that they can't be the absolute best they can be down there at the bottom."

STAR PRINCIPAL FOLLOWS PROVEN PATHWAY

Frank LeTreaux, principal of Smog-wheeze Middle School in Los Angeles, has resigned and taken a position as assistant vice president of human resources at Mattel, a toy manufacturer with over a billion dollars in annual revenue.

LeTreaux is, however, ambivalent about the move. "I don't really care about Mattel or the stuff it makes. Barbie? Hot Wheels? That's not my passion."

Instead, what brought LeTreaux to Mattel was a desire to become a school district superintendent. "I have it all planned out," he says. "I'll work at Mattel for 4 or 5 years, then I'll apply to the Broad Superintendents Academy, and from there I'll be eligible to get a nice position running a school district."

By standards that were used only a couple of decades ago, LeTreaux

... unless your self is a professional educator, of course.

already seems like a good candidate for such a position. After teaching for 8 years at an urban high school in New Haven, Connecticut, he earned a doctorate from Penn and came out to Los Angeles, where he's successfully led three different schools. But his career then stalled.

"I saw the handwriting on the wall. I'm too traditional. My teaching career, the PhD, the principalships—there's no way I'll ever get hired as a superintendent."

LeTreaux's plan is to take all the education work off his resume when he applies to the Broad Academy. "Since I was never TFA [Teach for America], they're more likely to accept me if they think I have only business experience," he explained.

HEATED BATTLE FOR "REFORMER" MANTLE

The past month has seen a marked intensification of the battle over who has the strongest claim to be called a "reformer."

The recent skirmish started in early December, when Kitty Wilson of Democrats Infatuated with Repub-

The delicate process of school reform.

lican Policies (DIRP) took the lead in the reformer battle with a bold proposal to level every public school in America with a bulldozer and then sow the ground with salt.

When told of that proposal, Gray P. Jean of the Brooklyn Institute said, "Oh yeah? Well, *we* propose that the schools be destroyed with bombs. Big ones. With lots of loud noise and stuff." Jean then added, "We'll set up a competitive system among the bombers, to ensure that the process is high-quality."

This healthy debate reflects enormous progress from a mere 2 decades ago, when people were most likely to be called reformers when they made proposals for school improvement grounded in research. Such people are now universally understood to be mere defenders of the status quo.

SCHOOL CHOICE

There is a real value in having choices, about such matters as procreation, laundry detergents, potential spouses, or schools. But sometimes choices cause harm to ourselves or other people, and sometimes additional choices add very little. Yes, we can buy either Simply Organic White Cheddar Doritos or Simply Organic Spicy White Cheddar Doritos. But how much has that made us better people or a better society?

My perspective is that fetishizing choice, or pursuing additional choice as a good in and of itself, can become problematic. So, for instance, while we tend to nod our heads when a politician says, "Nobody knows better what a child needs than that child's parents," we may stop nodding when we see the homeschooling approaches of neo-Nazi parents. (That's a real thing, sadly.) The next three articles don't explore that particular quandary, but they do have some fun with the choice über alles folks.

A CHILD'S SCHOOL IS THE CHILD'S CHOICE

This morning, Secretary of Education Betsy DeVos joined a coalition of school choice groups to announce a new campaign to empower children throughout the United States. The "A Child's School is the Child's Choice"

Potential Grizzlies, pages 13–17

campaign will hand school choice decisions from parents over to their children.

"For too long," said DeVos, "parents have stood between their children and the schools those children want to attend. A child's school should not be dictated by adults."

Coinciding with the launch, the school choice coalition released the results of a new survey of parents and their children. More than 58% of parent respondents voiced support for their kids "taking over the decision-making process" and agreed with the statement, "We have better things to do with our time."

Child respondents expressed enthusiasm about having a greater say in their own education. While only 16% embraced the idea of "researching different school options," an overwhelming 89% agreed that their parents were "totally clueless anyway."

At the press conference, DeVos introduced nine-year-old Damian

Studying for geometry class.

Scott, who told reporters, "Now I'll be able to switch schools when the teachers aren't being nice to me. Last year, I got a B in math. Secretary DeVos told me I was a victim of government Tyranny! She is a nice lady. She gave me cupcakes."

"Adults," DeVos explained, "are stuck in the past about what school could and should be, unwilling to experiment with new and exciting approaches."

That's not the case with children, she said:

> Kids know what they want. It might be a challenging curriculum grounded in engaging content and teaching approaches with strong supports and necessary resources. Or it might be making YouTube videos providing Tide Pod Challenge tutorials. But make no mistake: Absolutely nobody knows what a student needs to thrive better than that student—not the government and not the student's parents.

Past Proposal

The new "Child's Choice" campaign was also joined by the Association for Consumer Rights In Decisionmaking, which has long championed a version of the idea whereby educational funding is provided directly to the nation's children. ACRID's president Peter Knoll explained, "We currently spend about $10,000 per year on each child. We propose spending $5,000 instead, giving that money to the child—not to some bureaucrat."

Under the ACRID proposal, each child would be given about $28 in cash each day for 180 days a year. They would then choose where to buy their education that day—from any number of unregulated service providers.

"Let's say a kid starts his day with his $28 and decides to buy some language instruction in the morning and YouTube selfie-instruction videos in the afternoon, but has $6 left over after that," Knoll reasoned. "They can use that however they want to. That's a clear incentive to spend wisely!"

Among other options, children could choose to spend some of their allotment on afterschool snacks or invest it in hedge funds. "Schools are just going to have to make themselves more attractive and compete," said Knoll. "That's how markets work."

NEW STUDY LINKS TEACHER UNIONS TO SATAN

Confirming what many observers have long suspected, a leading think tank has shown that the devil is covertly in control of the nation's major teacher unions. "This fully explains why they oppose vouchers and merit pay. It's well-known that the Prince of Darkness has long held such policies in disfavor," explained Chester Gill, author of the study.

Standing between you and your vouchers.

Teacher unions, which defend the Status Quo of Sinfulness, have been aided by Satan in somehow causing the academic achievement of students receiving vouchers to fail to show improvement compared to public school students in study after study, according to Gill.

Although this reporter was not permitted to see the proof used in the study, readers should take Gill's word for it—just like we always do.

CHARTERING AUTHORITY GIVEN TO FAST FOOD CHAINS

Prospective charter school operators today touted a proposed new law allowing fast food restaurants to create and run new schools. The law's backers promise that it will open up exciting franchise opportunities, with the added bonus that the companies will be able to provide school meals and snacks.

Faculty meetings of the future.

Allen Jean, president of the advocacy group Charters Really Are Something Special (CRASS), asserted that the current state law is unfair because the authorization process can actually stop some people from starting up their own school. "If authorization is only available from organizations with experience with schools, there's nobody looking out for those without traditional qualifications," he explained, using air-quotes around the final word.

READING WARS

The so-called reading wars are mystifying to most of us. Why do some people so passionately embrace one particular way of teaching reading to children? These factions have even become identified with broader political positions, with advocates of a skills-based approach generally coming from more conservative perspectives, while advocates of a whole language approach come from more progressive political camps. While the latter group urges teachers to use literature and contextual understanding to engage children as life-long readers, the former urges explicit phonics lessons and sight word practice. In truth, most teachers and most people outside these two camps see real value in all of these instructional tools and want to see them broadly and appropriately used, in the hands of skilled educators. But we don't see such nuance in the heated battles of the reading wars.

GANG FIGHT SENDS READING SPECIALISTS TO HOSPITAL

Law enforcement is continuing its investigation of a gang fight between members of the Southside Phonics and the Outlaw Whole Languagers.

Sheriff Dibels said they had not yet decoded the series of events

When you're a Southside Phonics you're a Southside Phonics all the way.

leading up to the fight, but residents of nearby buildings reported hearing shouts back and forth that sounded like, "Emphasize meaning, motherf**kers!" and "Emphasize letter-to-sound correspondences, bitches!" Dibels also noted that the tensions between these rival gangs go back so far that nobody remembers the original cause of hostilities.

BILLIONAIRES AND THEIR BUDDIES

In addition to the aforementioned Eli Broad, billionaires have involved themselves to an astonishing degree in the education-reform realm. The Walton Family Foundation and individual billionaire Waltons (the Walmart fortune), Netflix founder Reed Hastings, and Facebook's Mark Zuckerberg, along with Michael Bloomberg and the Bill and Melinda Gates Foundation, have been among the most active. This billionaire engagement is probably best exemplified by the announcement by Zuckerberg on "Oprah" in 2010 of a $100 million gift to Newark Public Schools from himself and his wife, Priscilla Chan. They worked with then-mayor Cory Booker and then-governor Chris Christie to shape a charter-promoting, consultant-heavy vision of top-down reform that was later documented in the book, *The Prize*, by Dale Russakoff. Short version: mistakes were made.

Arne Duncan's $4.35 billion Race to the Top competitive grant program emerged concurrently, as part of the 2009 American Recovery and Reinvestment (Stimulus) Act. To access this federal money, states had to adopt policies favored by Duncan and the Obama administration, including removing limits on (and otherwise promoting) charter schools and using student test scores to evaluate teachers.

The following two articles were inspired by these developments, and later articles in this book occasionally return to these themes.

Potential Grizzlies, pages 21–24
Copyright © 2021 by Information Age Publishing

GATES FOUNDATION LAUNCHES
INNOVATIVE GRANTING INITIATIVE

The Gates Foundation has announced a compelling new experiment to test the hypothesis that any policy proposal, no matter how absurd, will be adopted by policymakers if enough money is dangled in front of them.

The initiative was inspired in part by game shows and in part by the federal Race to the Top program, which used the incentive of federal

Fidometry and trigodogometry class.

grants to persuade state legislators to adopt a variety of policies that they would otherwise have dismissed as rubbish.

The Foundation's first request for proposals is for introducing basset hounds as teachers in advanced math classes.

"Most states have already told us that they'll be submitting proposals," said Gates spokesperson Christine Jollity, "although some have asked for clarification about which math classes must be categorized as advanced. Apparently, they're really thinking it through, and they're seeing benefits in terms of addressing teacher shortages as well as salary savings."

"The time is right for this new granting initiative, given the combination of constrained public coffers and a lack of any guiding moral compass among so many of the nation's leaders. But honestly, we're just having fun," she explained. "We want to see how far policymakers will go before they tell us to fuck off."

BLOOMBERG ACQUIRES PARTIAL STAKE IN LAUSD

Back in the winter of 2017, when former New York Mayor Michael Bloomberg made a quick trip to Los Angeles to purchase a couple Bel Air mansions and ideological control over the city's school district, he may not have realized the long journey ahead.

After months of behind-the-scenes machinations that many market observers thought would lead to the full sale of the Los Angeles Unified School District to an investment group led by Bloomberg, the city's voters decided to hand over a mere partial stake. This setback notwithstanding, Bloomberg's spokesperson, Ollie Garkey, insists that further acquisitions in this and other districts will take place over the next several years.

"We have a long-term investment strategy," Garkey explained. "We expect to liquidate unproductive assets in the LAUSD, and we expect new investors to join our team." He added that Bloomberg and his allies are working hard to ensure devaluation of unacquired schools in districts throughout the U.S. marketplace.

"The problem, of course, is that the bidding procedure in school district 'elections' is too unpredictable," said Garkey. "How fair is it when

the high bidder is denied the purchase? Most investors are unwilling to enter a market with such high risk. As is, the system is unworkable and unacceptable. The entire investment community must now work together to design a more reliable election

Bloomberg and unnamed investor, possibly giving gang signs.

process and a more welcome marketplace for venture capitalists."

USC Football Option on Hold

Bloomberg's acquisition pushes aside, at least temporarily, the proposal to hand LAUSD over to the USC football program. An independent commission appointed last spring urged policymakers to consider that option.

"The mayor, the school board, the union, the superintendent, the charter operators—they're all part of the problem. We had nowhere else to turn," said commission chair Reggie Simpson, "USC football has shown that it can blatantly violate all the rules and come out on top. That sort of can-do, no-excuses spirit has been lacking in this district for as long as we can remember."

Other options had been considered by the commission but passed over. For instance, the *Los Angeles Times* had actively sought to have the district put under its supervision. The *Times* cited as experience its past efforts using astrologers to determine the quality of the district's teachers. But the commission was hesitant to turn the district over to a newspaper that would, in all likelihood, fold sometime around the second week of February.

New Potential Investor in Newark

Meanwhile, on the opposite coast, Mikhail Prokhorov, the Russian billionaire who formerly owned the New Jersey Nets basketball team, is entering the bidding war to control the state's embattled Newark school district. His spokesman hinted that Prokhorov, who built his fortune on the mining of nickel and precious metals, might go as high as $210 million, considerably more than the $100 million that Facebook's Mark Zuckerberg bid to acquire control in 2010.

Zuckerberg's plan for the district focused on his love of charter schools and his belief that grades should be based on the student's number of "likes." Prokhorov, however, apparently wants to push the district toward metal mining.

When asked for their views on the possible shift in their overseers, Newark residents expressed shock and asked if under the new ownership someone might actually care if they have views.

THOSE DREADFUL TEACHERS

Before the coronavirus crisis provided parents and others with the insight that teaching is somewhat difficult and that teachers need supports more than ridicule, the nation experienced a prolonged era of teacher bashing. My pieces examined that, as well as a smorgasbord of reformy nonsense peddled by advocacy think tanks. The following eight articles were particularly inspired by teacher-evaluation schemes, such as the idea of evaluating teachers based on their students' test scores, and then dismissing and replacing the bottom five percent of teachers. If you find yourself confused by any of these articles, I suggest that the blame must lie with your third grade teacher.

BUMPS ON HEAD KEY TO NEW TEACHER QUALITY MODEL

A new study by the National Center for Quality Teaching shows that the quality of potential teachers may be determined by the nature of bumps on their skulls rather than (as some had erroneously assumed) by training and experience.

"All this time the true measure of teaching quality has only been a caliper away," said Cindy Walls,

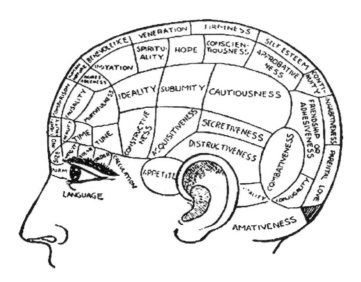

Good teaching is based on good science.

President of NCQT, while pointing to a phrenological diagram of Jaime Escalante's "perfect teacher" head. Walls said that this study is the nail in the coffin of the "credentialists." "For years, they've told us that teachers should be 'trained' and 'educated' and 'prepared.' What charlatans!"

ARSE GIVES TEACHER QUALITY RANKINGS FIRST PLACE

The respected group Absurd Ratings of Schooling Endeavors (ARSE) has given the coveted "F–" rank to the National Council on Quality Teaching. The F– is actually the highest rating given by ARSE, an approach it adopted when it discovered the direct relationship between negative ratings and increased media coverage. "The research evidence clearly indicates that the only way to ensure success is by declaring failure," said ARSE director Rose Bumm.

Winning at failing.

"It's all part of the game," said Bumm. "The think tank does its part by assigning eye-catching grades, and the press run with the story. It's win-win. And nobody does it better than our friends at the NCQT."

The deciding factor in favor of the NCQT, which advocates innovative ways of undermining teacher educa-tion, was that their rankings gave no state a grade higher than a C–. "They simply did the best job of arbitrary castigation," said Bumm.

In a world where any two people with a 501(c)(3) and a press release can issue grades that reflect and promote their agenda, ARSE was formed to assure quality control. ARSE standards demand a combination of non-comparable measures, arbitrary weights, and narrow and invalid measures.

URBAN BUILDINGS TO BE CLOSED:
LOW TEST SCORES CITED

New Jersey Governor Chris Christie today unveiled his administration's Blame Our Buildings (BOB) act, an ambitious plan to turn around the state's chronically underperforming urban school buildings.

Bad.

The governor explained that unionized teachers are not the only ones at fault for student failure; blame also extends to the physical buildings. "Our careful, value-added analyses show that student growth in some of these buildings is abysmal," said Christie. "If we close all urban schools, we can get rid of buildings that are old, expensive to maintain, and just plain bad."

In place of the closed buildings, the state will contract with a private, for-profit company to provide urban students with an online, virtual education. Students will be required to peck at a button on the keyboard every 60 seconds, in order to ensure that they are present and paying attention. "Not only will BOB close the dropout factories," Christie enthused, "it will effectively put the little thugs under house arrest."

TEST MAKERS TO BE EVALUATED ON STUDENTS' TEST SCORES

Citing years of stagnant test scores, Tennessee's legislature and governor have revised the state's assessment policy. Starting next year, the state will hold the developers of its standardized tests accountable for increasing students' test scores.

"If you look across the U.S., you see a kind of 'widget effect,' where every company making standardized tests is evaluated as successful," said Gov. Bill Lee. "But we know they can't all be successful, because we can see that our students aren't doing nearly well enough on those tests."

In fact, research has found substantial variation among these tests, with students consistently showing more growth on some tests than others. This variation will allow for Tennessee to hold lower-performing assessments accountable, while al-

It's stressful for these students to know that the test-maker's fate lies in their hands.

lowing the high-flyers to rise to the top.

Critics of the approach warned that the test makers will find ways to game the system to ensure that students show growth. "They'll start to test to the test," predicted educational historian Diane Ravitch.

TEACHER EFFECTIVENESS LINKED TO HEIGHT

A new study offers conclusive proof that tall teachers are more effective teachers. Using sophisticated statistical modeling techniques, researcher Tom Able showed that if the least effective (aka shortest) teachers were removed from the teaching ranks at a rate of just seven percent each year and were replaced by teachers with just average effectiveness (approximately 5' 4.5" tall for women and 5' 10" tall for men), within a decade American teacher quality would be among the best in the world.

Only one of these gentlemen will make a good teacher.

"The key element of this study," explained Able, "was our ability at the outset to conclusively define teachers' effectiveness as equivalent to their height, before we even started looking at the data. Once we figured that out, the rest was easy because there is substantial variation in teachers' height and, unlike other possible measures of teacher quality, adult height is very, very stable over time."

Able added that the less effective teachers are easily defined as the shorter teachers—who the study definitively shows are shorter. If those teachers are replaced by more effective teachers—the taller teachers who the study shows are definitively taller—the result is very clearly that the average teaching force becomes more effective, since they're taller.

"The beauty of this research," Able said, "is that I'm pretty sure we could also improve teachers' effectiveness this way if we were to use their hair color, age, or even their students' value-added test scores. All we have to do is make sure our outcome measure of teacher effectiveness is the same thing we're manipulating in our models."

BOTTOM FIVE PERCENT OF ECONOMISTS FACE DISMISSAL

Responding to the crisis of failed policies recommended by the nation's economists, a consortium of universities and think tanks have agreed to annually fire the bottom five percent of economists.

"If there's one thing we know, it's that economists are the most important factor in the success of our nation's lawmakers," explained Mary Barth, the consortium's leader. "We can no longer simply ignore the bad economists. The stakes are too high."

Barth acknowledged that year-to-year changes in policy are influenced by overall conditions in the nation as well as by lawmakers. "Those are things we don't have control over," she explained. "And we won't let the defenders of the status quo point to those other factors to make excuses for the bad economists."

By focusing on the quality of economists, the consortium contends it can incrementally develop one of the finest policy-analyst corps in the world. Even if those who are fired are replaced by only mediocre economists, the overall level of advice should substantially increase after just a few years.

"Research has shown that a lawmaker who receives just 3 years of advice from a low-performing economist will muck up a substantially greater amount of policy than her colleague who receives advice from just an average economist," said Barth.

Nevertheless, the Union of American Economists is opposing the consortium's improvement efforts, denouncing the new policy as unfair to its members.

"This policy creates perverse incentives for economists, pushing them to focus on policy areas with less need, but which are likely to see improvement even if it's due to factors far beyond the scope of the economists' advice," said UAE director John Kyle. "The most challenging policy areas will be left only to those economists with no other options."

Kyle also warned that the policy would cast a pall over the entire profession, with otherwise-creative economists becoming unwilling to

Will accountability cast a pall over economists?

offer new ideas.

Barth counters that this resistance to accountability is to be expected, and she vows to fight the entrenched interests. Economists, she pointed out, are among the few professionals not judged by their performance. "The coddling," she said, "must end."

New Standards for Economists

This new policy was announced at a particularly eventful time for the field of economics. Just last week, the new Standards for Economists (4th Edition) were published by the Society of Misleading Ivory Tower Economists (SMITE). Pursuant to those Standards, studies should be "based on a model that has no actual connection to the real world but nonetheless arrives at findings that are clear and definite."

The rules, which codify long-accepted practice, were met with wide praise. "Elegance is found in the model itself," said Richard Luke of the University of Chicago, the current president of SMITE. "The real world is ugly and messy—it's not elegant at all. We should never waste time trying to understand it. And we should certainly never let it sully our beautiful models."

Leaders in the field are unsure how these standards will interact with the "bottom five percent" policy. "These are uncertain times," said Luke. "Who knows what will happen if we have incentives to be accountable."

NEW BOTTOM 5% OF TEACHERS MYSTERIOUSLY APPEAR AFTER OLD ONES ARE FIRED

A new study published by Harvard economist Betty Raj describes an enigmatic flaw in her otherwise perfect scheme for improving teacher quality. According to the article, Los Diablos Unified School District (Raj's pseudonym for the district) used value-added modeling to determine teachers' impact on students' test scores. Then, as called for in Raj's plan, the district fired the bottom-performing five percent of the teachers and hired new teachers.

The march of progress.

To everyone's surprise, the following year a new group of teachers emerged who, just like the prior year, were measured to be in the bottom five percent. According to the study, the same phenomenon occurred during the third year.

"We checked the data to make sure that those bad teachers were not sneaking back into the district," wrote Raj. "That did not appear to be the case. We did, however, discover that the new bottom group of teachers was packed with those who were newly hired and those teaching in the same schools as those who were fired, so maybe they re-entered under assumed names."

District officials voiced confidence that the glitch will disappear over time. "We'll just keep firing them. Sooner or later, it'll stick!"

OUT-OF-FIELD DOCTORING ADDRESSED
BY "OPERATE FOR AMERICA"

Local hospitals announced today that they are signing on with "Operate

Enthusiasm and energy are vitally important for surgeons.

for America," a new program that provides hospitals in low-income communities with college graduates whose zeal, vigor, and youth will more than make up for their lack of qualifications and experience.

The influx of new talent allows hospitals to minimize out-of-field doctoring and the use of "long-term substitute" surgeons. According to a recent study, neurosurgery in lower-income communities has often been performed by doctors trained as dermatologists. The study also found multiple instances of cardiac surgery by podiatrists.

The OFA workers all get 5 weeks of intensive training the summer before they begin performing surgery.

DEREGULATION, CRISIS, AND CLOSURE

As illustrated by many of the above articles, a recurring contention over the past couple of decades has been that the public schools are "failing" and that this crisis necessitates radical change, usually in the form of privatization and deregulation. The following four articles further develop these ideas.

OPEN LETTER FROM *EdTweak* TO THE NEXT PRESIDENT

It is with utmost respect that we urge you to fully commit yourself to using the power of the unregulated marketplace to drive school reform. Just because less regulation and a freer market didn't work out especially well for airlines, the energy industry, banks and savings and loans, telecommunications, and health care doesn't mean we shouldn't give it a shot for the education of our children.

As an important first step, we urge you to close down government schools. That is, we discourage a so-called "public option." Supporters of a public schooling option are socialists and even scallywags. Only private companies should run schools, and they should be paid based entirely on student test scores. This gives us a measurable output that can be commodified and thereby allow the free

Potential Grizzlies, pages 35–39
Copyright © 2021 by Information Age Publishing

Pharma Bro Martin Shkreli, Enron's Jeffrey Skilling, and U.S. Education Secretary Betsy DeVos warn that creativity and innovation are stifled by government regulation.

market to work its magic.

Specifically, new companies would sprout up not only to run these schools but to create a secondary market for the test score payments. We envision a National Overvalued Score Exchange (NOSE) that would allow investors to determine the true worth of students and their scores. In fact, the scores could be packaged in new, inventive ways for trading, with test-score futures, options and derivatives to facilitate the buying and selling of risk.

The federally authorized Score Hazard Trading Insurance Corporation (SHTIC)—or even the Treasury itself—could step in, if things get out of hand. But why worry? If nothing else, any failure of this system will likely be big enough to have international repercussions, bringing those pesky, high-scoring Singaporeans and Canadians down with us.

CHICAGO, PHILADELPHIA SCHOOLS
CLOSED FOR SNOW JOB

A giant snow-job system reaching across a wide swath of the country is threatening to close dozens of schools in Chicago and Philadelphia, forecasters announced this afternoon. Schools in New York City and Washington DC are also under threat.

"This is part of an ongoing, relentless system," said Belinda Gateswalton-Broad, a professional education disrupter. "There is nothing to stop it, or at least that's what we're counting on."

In Philadelphia last week, teachers and supporters were seen shoveling away part of the latest snow job. Several were arrested while mounting a protest against the snow job.

"Who knows when the snow job will end?" said Marsha Jones, a fifth-grade teacher hidden deep within her snow bunker. "The excitement of a

Marsha Jones waits out the latest snow job.

snow-job day is maybe a little fun at first. But I'd like to get back to teaching kids."

CHICAGO WINS LATEST DEPARTMENT OF EDUCATION COMPETITION

Education Secretary Arne Duncan announced today that he has awarded Chicago Public Schools $18 million in the first round of the "Race to Demoralize" competition. While school districts from across the United States have been working hard to undermine their community's trust, Chicago's effort rose to the bottom.

The prize committee praised the district's delightfully disheartening decision to close 49 schools, but the victory still came as a bit of a surprise. New Orleans was thought by many to be the frontrunner in the competition but appears to have lost out because of confusion about whether the city still has a public school district.

"CPS has shown its steadfast dedication to disregarding the people they nominally serve, refusing to bow to the special interests such as children, parents, and teachers," proclaimed Duncan at the announcement ceremony.

When a Chicago parent asked whether the $18 million awarded to CPS will be sufficient to repair all the damage done by the closures, Duncan pointed out that the grant is not intended to be used to help the students or the schools. Instead, it will be earmarked to hire a team of public relations experts who will find creative ways to explain the benevolence of the district leadership to parents and students.

255 DROP OUT EACH MINUTE, SAYS NEW REPORT

The Association for Scary Statistics today released a study projecting that more than 16.5 million students—about 255 per minute—will drop out

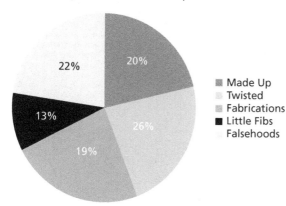

of high school this academic year.

"That's based on a 180-day school year and a 6-hour school day," explained ASS spokesperson Roger Grant. Asked why ASS's estimate is significantly higher than any other seen to date, Grant said, "We started with the highest drop-out rate estimate we could find, but we thought it looked a little too optimistic, so we adjusted for that, and then of course adjusted that result by the percentage decline in the S&P 500 during the bear market in early 2020."

Commenting on the study, Barry Jones of the Policy Institute of Economics pointed out that if 16.5 million students really did drop out each year, the nation's high schools would soon be completely empty. Replied Grant, "I'm afraid Barry is in denial about the magnitude of this crisis."

PARENT TRIGGER

The so-called Parent Trigger law arose in California about a decade ago as a policy darling of charter-school advocates—particularly a group called Parent Revolution. It required school districts to convert low-scoring schools into charter schools if at least half of the school's parents signed a petition asking the district to do so. Although this has only been successfully done once over those 10 years, the idea itself captured a great deal of attention. The following two pieces develop the idea a bit further.

PARENT TRIGGER PROPOSAL WOULD CONVERT FAILING CHARTERS INTO UNIONIZED NEIGHBORHOOD SCHOOLS

At a time when lawmakers are searching for ways to drive change and empower parents, a new proposal would allow California parents to seize charter schools and turn those schools into neighborhood schools, controlled by democratically elected school boards, with unionized teachers.

The proposal builds on the state's existing Parent Trigger law, which allows 51% of parents at schools with low test scores to force a district to turn that school over to a charter school operator. But according to

Potential Grizzlies, pages 41–43
Copyright © 2021 by Information Age Publishing

New Parent Trigger organizer Sue Meyers, that law does not go far enough. "What about parents in communities served by low-performing charter schools? We need help, too."

"Our charter is awful," Meyers said. "Teachers come and go before we even know who they are. Decisions are made by the school's cor-

The New Parent Trigger proposal still awaits support from parental-choice funders.

porate headquarters in Chicago. They

have no teachers prepared to help with special needs kids or English learners."

Meyers spoke last night to a gathering of other concerned parents. "Why do parents have to stand idly by?" she asked. "Why can't we have high-achieving, unionized schools like the rich people across town?"

Meyers says that New Parent Trigger is currently struggling to get financial backing. "We sought funding from the Gates, Broad, and Walton Foundations, all of which generously supported the initial parent trigger policy initiatives. But they turned us down. I don't understand why they don't want to support us as well. Am I missing something? After all, a choice is a choice."

TEACHERS FACE CALIFORNIA'S STUDENT TRIGGER LAW

Beginning next month, any child in a failing classroom will be able to remove her teacher by collecting signatures from 51% of the class's students.

"For the first time anywhere in America, students have been empowered, entrusted with the legal right to force dramatic change in their failing classrooms," said Ben Starr, the director of Student Revolution, the group behind the new law. "Our opponents issued dire warnings of unintended consequences. But we've already tried out the approach in two small districts, and we've seen an enormous increase in teachers' effort and effectiveness. In fact, students' grades have skyrocketed!"

Student Revolution, which we in

The straw poll is not looking good for Ms. Peters.

the press have been instructed to call a "grassroots popular movement," was founded last year by visionary billionaires.

BUDGET REDUCTION

Quoting C-SPAN: "The Joint Select Committee on Deficit Reduction, colloquially referred to as the Supercommittee, was a joint select committee of the United States Congress, created by the Budget Control Act of 2011 on August 2, 2011 . . . The objective of the committee was to develop a deficit reduction plan over 10 years in addition to the $917 billion of cuts and initial debt limit increase of $900 billion in the Budget Control Act of 2011 that avoided a U.S. sovereign default."

That was the context for the following piece, but the main motivation was the amusing but pathetic negotiation process that appeared to involve little more than a string of concessions from Congressional Democrats.

BUDGET COMMITTEE SETTLES ON TAX HIKES FOR THIRD GRADERS

Children attending third grade in America's public schools will bear the brunt of a compromise plan ironed out by the Joint Select Committee on Deficit Reduction, referred to as the "Super Committee" of the U.S. Congress. Over the next decade, the children will each be asked to pay a one-time tax of $50,000 upon their third-grade enrollment, generating about $200 billion annually.

Sources close to the negotiations

Potential Grizzlies, pages 45–46

described how committee members were divided along party lines, with Democrats wanting to tax seventh graders and Republicans wanting to tax second graders. Likewise, Democrats wanted to tax all students, including those enrolled in private and parochial school, while Republicans wanted to tax only public school students—as reflected in the final agreement.

"We got them to move on the second-grade issue," declared an obviously pleased Sen. Patty Murray (D–WA). Meanwhile, Republican leaders expressed concern that the move from second-graders to third-graders would be unacceptable to many members of their caucus.

After months of give and take, the congressional negotiators decided that a tax on schoolchildren made more sense than taxing the wealthy. "There are over four million third graders in public schools, but there are only three million Americans in the top one percent," explained Sen. Patrick J. Toomey (R–PA). "It just makes sense to share the burden."

Many specifics of the final legislation have yet to be ironed out. But one key element will be a federal guarantee given to financial institutions willing to make the risky personal loans that will be necessary in order for the nation's lower-income third graders to assume their fair share of the national debt.

Rep. Fred Upton (R–MI) pointed out that third graders are an untapped resource, rarely contributing directly to the economy. "My experience has been that these youth squander their energies on unproductive activities, often engaging in kickball and drawing and whatnot. The compromise makes reasonable demands, constituting only a small portion of the overall personal indebtedness they will have incurred by their early thirties."

Bobby's doing his part.

CLASS SIZE

During congressional testimony in 2019, Secretary DeVos said, "Students may be better served by being in larger classes, if by hiring fewer teachers, a district or state can better compensate those who have demonstrated high quality and outstanding results." She added, "Some students can learn better with larger classes with more students to collaborate with, to learn with." The rest of the following piece is self-explanatory (the information about their children's schools is correct).

CLASS SIZES WILL BE "THE BIGGEST EVER," BOASTS PRESIDENT TRUMP

Doubling down on Education Secretary Betsy DeVos' recent claim that "some students can learn better with larger classes, with more students to collaborate with, to learn with," President Trump this morning bragged that the United States will soon lead the world in class size. "Under President Trump, our classes will be huge. They'll be the biggest, most beautiful class sizes you've ever seen, believe me!"

"I guarantee you," he added, "there's no problem"—leaving the audience a bit confused.

The president then blasted what he called the "pathetic, sad class sizes of lightweight" past presidents. "A lot of

Potential Grizzlies, pages 47–48
Copyright © 2021 by Information Age Publishing
All rights of reproduction in any form reserved.

47

people are saying that we have low-energy students with low-energy teachers," he continued. "Look at China and Mexico with their tremendous

Also, immigrants are to blame.

class sizes. They're laughing at us."

But with "class sizes like never seen before, ever, we'll beat those choker countries like a dog. Our puny class sizes don't stand a chance with me as your favorite President!"

The President then launched into a rousing speech that left his audience cheering, "Grow the Class! Grow the Class!"

The president didn't mention whether he would pull his son from St. Andrews, which has a far-too-small median class size of 15 and a 7:1 student to teacher ratio. Secretary DeVos sent her two sons to Grand Rapids Christian High School, which boasts an average class size of only 24, so they were sadly deprived of great opportunities to collaborate and learn.

STRATIFIED OPPORTUNITY

Dating back to its 1787 Constitution, the United States has always been impressive in its ability to find new and creative ways to perpetuate inequalities. The following two stories explore one little slice of that: how we stratify opportunities within schools.

WEALTHY WHITE PUPILS RELINQUISH SOME EXECUTIVE PERKS

In a move designed to appease their plebeian colleagues, the wealthy White students at Brynleigh High School have agreed to give up some of their executive perks. The decision to part with their elegant catered meals and memberships in the school's exclusive social club was prompted by the other students' brief strike last month, during which they refused to clean the executive washrooms used by their elite brethren.

As part of the negotiated compromise, wealthy White pupils will retain exclusive rights to the school's experienced teachers and its Advanced Placement program.

Hailee Heath, who was briefly forced to pick up a mop during the uprising, was satisfied with the reso-

lution and is hopeful that this nasty business is settled. "This whole thing came as a surprise, since they always seemed happy and had never really complained before. We only want the best for them."

Hailee Heath, during the dark days.

UNGIFTED TO USE FEWER RESOURCES

After careful study, an Aislada School District task force has concluded that quality education is a limited resource and that students with no giftedness are simply receiving too much of it. The district immediately sent a letter to the parents of ungifted students, explaining that in the future other students will be getting the school's best educational opportunities.

As the letter explains to the ungifted parents, "This upcoming year, we will provide excellent gifted programs for our more talented students, which does not include your child. As we are sure you'll understand, your child would not benefit from these outstanding programs, since he or she is not gifted."

The letter also describes the learning resources that the other students will receive: "They will be exposed to exciting, hands-on learning experiences, undisturbed by ungifted students. This will give tomorrow's leaders skills and talents that your child simply will not need and could not properly exercise."

Michael is wonderfully gifted, unlike Gloria.

The district hasn't yet decided upon the nature of the instruction to be provided in the classrooms for the ungifted children. "We're thinking maybe worksheets, combined with some P.E. But let's be honest—it really doesn't matter."

GROWTH MINDSET

Carol Dweck, a professor of psychology at Stanford University, has long written about what she calls two basic mindsets: a belief that one's own capacities for learning and achieving on any given task are set (a "fixed mindset," a conviction that some people are innately smart while others are stupid), or a belief that a person can put in the time and effort to improve and achieve (a "growth mindset"). This idea of a growth mindset is very reasonable and can be helpful in approaching teaching and learning. But, as Dweck herself has pointed out, the popularity of the idea has led to superficial spin-offs and misunderstandings. In fact, in the worst case, the idea is used for blaming students rather than teaching them ("Chris and Megan failed this test because they didn't work hard enough."). The below piece was written as a response to the popularity of growth-mindset jargon, often combined with superficial professional development and student assemblies.

NASTY-LOOKING GROWTH SPOTTED ON MINDSET

Gwen Cooper, a 12 year old attending Bear Basin Middle School, became alarmed this morning when her friends noticed an unsightly growth on her mindset. "Until today, my mindset has always been brilliant,"

Potential Grizzlies, pages 53–54
Copyright © 2021 by Information Age Publishing
All rights of reproduction in any form reserved.

complained Cooper. "I was born en-
dowed with one of the best mindsets
in the state. My parents have always
told me that."

Alison Cooper, Gwen's mother,
confirmed that a flawless mindset
always came naturally
to her daughter. "Some
people just have it,
or at least that's what
I thought until today.
But oh my! What's that
dreadful growth she's
now burdened with?"

Gwen is not sure of
her next steps. "Hon-
estly, I don't know
what to do," she told us. "Maybe
through effort, perseverance, and
hard work I can fix my mindset and
get rid of the growth."

SCREEN TIME

A mong the marketizing crowd, one of the most attractive prospects in education is the possibility that the United States (and other nations) might replace brick-and-mortar schools with virtual or online education ("cyberschools"). The largest purveyor of online curriculum is K12 Inc., a for-profit company that contracts with charter schools across the country, sometimes providing only curriculum and sometimes running the school. The rhetorical advocacy from K12 Inc. and others is grounded in the idea of "personalization"—meaning that the software on the children's computer is responsive to what those children need at any given time. For example, if a student shows a misunderstanding of the Pythagorean theorem, such as failing to recognize the need for a right angle, the software focuses on teaching for that specific understanding. Ideally, everything runs smoothly in this brave new world, and everyone wins. In practice, students regularly flounder. As we have seen throughout the remote-learning, COVID-19 era, most students benefit substantially from their relationships with teachers and from the social learning environment of schools. Several of the below articles explore these issues.

The exception is the second article, which is lighthearted, not critical. It concerns the trendy embrace of the idea of a "flipped classroom." At its core, the idea merely proposes that teacher lectures be recorded and then watched

Potential Grizzlies, pages 55–62

by students at home, so that classroom time can be spent discussing the ideas. While there are problems with this (such as uneven lecture-watching among students), the piece I wrote was really just having a bit of fun.

REFORMERS TACKLE DEFICIENCY IN CHILDREN'S SCREEN TIME

Pointing to children's failure to spend adequate time in front of video screens, advocates of digital learning have proposed a package of reforms designed to increase youth awareness that time spent on books, recreation, and face-to-face interactions should be limited.

"While it's true that teenagers are averaging 6.5 hours of screen time a

You're not fooling us, Mr. Vincent.

day outside of school, some children spend literally hours at a time playing outside with friends or curled up reading by the fire in a comfy armchair," warned Anne Avatar, spokesperson for the Institute for Disruptive Innovation (IDI).

Avatar conceded that schools have limited capacity to directly address the problem of children who receive less than the recommended 6-hour dosage per day of screen time in their homes. But she contended that schools still have an important role to play. "While we can do little to intervene with neglectful parenting, we have a responsibility to ensure thorough screen-time immersion when children are in the care of our public schools. It's so sad to see children missing out on so much software."

To address this screen-time deficiency, IDI has rolled out an initiative that provides online curriculum from the moment a child enters a school building. Even children who get the 6-hour minimum outside of school will, Avatar explains, benefit tremendously from the new digital-learning plan. "Many children have now advanced to the stage where it is no longer feasible for them to interact with other people. Our schools are wasting the potential of these children, who could be learning through computers instead of staring blankly at a teacher lacking any obvious interface."

INTRODUCING THE FLIPPED-OFF CLASSROOM

Children across the United States have been celebrating the latest education trend, known as the flipped-off classroom. Instead of being well-behaved during class and then letting off steam on the playground or after school, obscene and previously inappropriate verbal and non-verbal communication is encouraged as part of healthy classroom discussions.

"We discovered that teachers were wasting precious learning time suppressing natural expression and emotion, which is just fucked up," said Harlan Jones, one of the movement's most enthusiastic leaders. "And we noticed that students were restless, fidgety, and even passionless—all because we were imposing unnatural constraints on their expressions."

Indeed, early evidence about the

reform suggests that participating children are less likely to have pent-up aggressions that they release as anti-social behaviors during unsupervised times.

Jones explained that the flipped-off classroom brings schooling in line with the rest of people's lives, helping children prepare for the workplace. "Visit a law office. Head down to the shop floor. Heck, drop by the fucking teachers' lounge! This is how real people communicate."

REFORMERS AUTOMATE PERSONALIZATION

In a breakthrough comparable to Socrates's first interactions with market goers in the agora, education's top innovators have succeeded

Move along, Bessie.

in creating personalized education but without the persons. From this point forward, America's youth will advance through school efficiently, in much the same way a cow advances through a modern abattoir, receiving only corrective guidance if they momentarily veer off track.

The fully automated personalization is made possible by advances in digital technology, with continuous online assessments of students. "Teaching is really just a form of marketing, and as with all great marketing, the learning through this software is micro-targeted, based on individualized data," explains Mark Vander Venal of the Parsimony Institute. "Under optimal conditions, the efficiency improvements have been measured at 46.12%."

For years, reformers have been calling for the next generation of schools to be more efficient, and they have focused on minimizing spending on teachers and other humans. Vander Venal, in announcing the culmination of the project, heaped praise on "the vision and tireless efforts of those dreamers."

Like players advancing through a video game by satisfactorily killing vampires or ethnic minorities, children advance through the curriculum by convincing the computer that they are proficient at the current level. Each computer terminal is colorfully labelled as, for example, *Third Grade* or *Fourth Grade*. The instructional software, in a major advance over past attempts at automated personalization, determines readiness for the child to move to the next level, all without human intervention.

Going by the name, "competency-based education," the system sorts students into their own individual pathways toward graduation.

"We chose these words very carefully," says Vander Venal. "After all, who could be against something called competency-based education?

And I remember when I first suggested using *personalization*, everyone laughed and said it wouldn't work.

They said that reporters and policymakers would see right through it. But who's laughing now?"

ACTUAL BULLY TARGETS STUDENTS AT VIRTUAL SCHOOL

Cosmo Paine is charting a new path for bullying.

Local bully Cosmo Paine is modifying his array of tormenting skills in preparation for his transfer from Euclid Middle School to Inert Online Academy.

"One must put aside the conventional physical approaches and develop a more nuanced set of tools in their place," the 13-year-old menace explained. "Social media, of course, must be mastered. But we mustn't discount the continuing importance of more direct threats and insults."

Concerns, however, were expressed by some older bullies. "The craft is quickly being lost," one told us. "Can any online performance match the elegance and tradition of wedgies, swirlies, Chinese burns, and 'Kick Me' signs?"

VIRTUAL CHARTER SCHOOL SUCCESSFULLY WOOS NEW HQ FOR INNOVATIVE, RESULTS-ORIENTED INTERNATIONAL INDUSTRY

In a move expected to boost its share prices, P12 Inc. (NYSE: SPRN) has reached a tentative agreement to house the headquarters of NPES Alliance, the umbrella industry association for Nigerian Prince email scamming.

NPES Alliance members generally reach out to their customer base via correspondence that "offers the recipient the 'opportunity' to share in a percentage of millions of dollars that the author—a self-proclaimed government official—is trying to transfer illegally out of Nigeria," according

Opportunity.

to the FBI. The recipient ultimately is convinced by the Alliance member to send money "in several installments of increasing amounts for a variety of reasons." Overall, this nets millions of dollars each year, although industry leaders are somewhat reticent to

confirm particulars, citing proprietary techniques that provide a competitive advantage.

P12 Inc. is an education management organization (EMO) that sells online schooling and curricula for public school students from preschool to 12th grade, reaching its customer base via advertisements on children's television, billboards, and bus-stop benches. Its business model has shown enormous success in acquiring legislator assets at reasonable prices, while generating moderate to severe adverse impacts on students' learning. The company last year reported a profit of over $30 million.

Moving NPES Alliance headquarters to Virginia will allow the two industries to jointly recruit and retain talent in the area. "It's a smart way for us to hire employees that fit what we're trying to do, from a business point of view," explained NPES's CEO in an email that added a plea for help in accessing some "trapped" funds. He also noted the fraud-friendly environment in nearby Washington, DC.

These positive sentiments were

echoed by Tom Slackard, P12 Inc.'s founder, who expounded on the opportunities that Alliance members will find throughout the country. "Their industry is built on outrageous promises that will go unfulfilled. But just as soon as one customer is disappointed, another comes along," he said. "It's an unbeatable formula for success."

MOOCs

A higher-education strain of the online-education mania is known as the MOOC (Massive Open Online Course). Through partnerships between universities and companies like Coursera and edX, anyone with a computer and internet access can "take" a course. The basic course is free, but a credential or the ability to, for example, ask the professor a question generally requires the paid version. MOOCs, we were told back in 2013 (when I wrote the following piece), would revolutionize higher education.

BOOCs: A GAME CHANGER

In a clear sign that seismic shifts in the education industry are about to occur, top Silicon Valley entrepreneurs have begun investing heavily in BOOC learning platforms.

The basic idea is simple and elegant. It begins when a person writes down ideas, information, stories, equations—almost anything really. Then another person prints out copies of that content, in BOOC form, and makes it widely available. Conceivably, these BOOCs may someday be accessed through the Internet.

"We think these BOOCs can be a major disrupter to old ways of learning," said Beck Tubble, one of the early investors. The innovators behind the BOOC idea came up with the name BOOC last year, which is

Potential Grizzlies, pages 63–64
Copyright © 2021 by Information Age Publishing

an acronym for Big Outrageously Original Concept.

As the industry develops, Tubble

The president is such a fan of BOOCs that he was willing to violently disperse crowds, just to gain access to this new technology.

explained, the investors envision BOOCs containing massive amounts of information that people across the globe will be able to access. Some BOOCs will even be made available, on a trial basis, in non-English languages.

There is also talk of creating institutions that would allow people to borrow BOOCs without charge—essentially free access to this knowledge. The current thinking is that these institutions would be called "libraries," in honor of the ancient Library of Alexandria, an earlier experiment with this exciting concept.

If the idea catches on, Tubble predicts people sharing ideas from BOOCs through clubs, "chats" in coffee houses, and exchanging BOOCs with friends and coworkers just as people now exchange links and retweet each other.

"This is the first learning platform we're aware of that allows people in the remotest places on earth to gain access to the world's knowledge," said Tubble. "It does away with the need for classrooms or conversations with teachers. Everything anyone will ever want to know will be in a BOOC, and all at very little cost—until we're ready to make a handsome profit, of course."

HIGHER ED GRADE INFLATION

STUDENT GROUP ADVOCATES GRADE INFLATION

"I just can't believe my psych professor!" said John Sawyer, leader of an ad hoc student group that meets in the wee hours of the morning at the Guzzling Yak bar near Cronus College. "I bought the textbook and even came to class most days, and he has the nerve to fail me!"

Sawyer says he enrolled in the psychology class because its meeting time fit well into his skiing schedule and wasn't in the morning. But he found some of it interesting and "kind of wanted to learn more, but not if the profs are going to be so anal about assignments."

His group, which calls itself "Students Wanting Inflated Grades" (SWIG), is generally made up of lackluster students who drink in

Exam Prep at the Guzzling Yak.

lieu of studying. But there are a few

Potential Grizzlies, pages 65–66
Copyright © 2021 by Information Age Publishing

exceptions. One of these is Madeline Thomas, who sat nursing a tall glass of beer next to Sawyer. She decided to attend her first SWIG meeting after unfair treatment by a mathematics professor.

"You know, sometimes professors are just too hard on us, for no apparent reason," Thomas explained. "Like my calculus instructor. My final grade in her class was 87, which is just a few points short of an A–. I sent her a very sweet email asking if I could do anything, anything at all, to raise it just a little bit, so I could have all A's on my transcript. And she just wouldn't do it. I mean what's a few points to her? It's pretty irrational, and even mean. Is that what I pay my tuition for?"

GUNS

During her senate confirmation hearing, education secretary nominee Betsy DeVos was asked her views on schools keeping guns on site. She responded to a question from a Wyoming senator with the insight that a rural elementary school in that state might do so: "I think probably there, I would imagine that there's probably a gun in the school to protect from potential grizzlies." Perhaps because this rationale was held up as making some sort of case for the larger pro-arming-teachers position, or perhaps because of the turn of the phrase itself, the "potential grizzlies" argument captured the nation's attention—or at least mine.

SECRETARY DEVOS HAS SECRET MEETING WITH POTENTIAL GRIZZLY

As part of Education Secretary Betsy DeVos's campaign to promote educational vouchers, she held a secret meeting last week with Boo Boo Medvedev, a Russian bear said to have close ties to bear leadership throughout the northern hemisphere.

Tensions between the two camps had flared following reports that DeVos had urged American teachers to open fire on members of the bear community. As a result, the powerful bear lobby had threatened to maul politicians who pretended not to

Potential Grizzlies, pages 67–69

know about recent studies of vouchers in Louisiana, Ohio, Indiana, and the District of Columbia, all showing

negative test score effects—in some cases, surprisingly large. This appeared to be a not-so-subtle reference to DeVos herself.

An education department spokesperson announced on Friday that the talks were very successful at de-escalating the situation. "The secretary explained to Mr. Medvedev that her statements had been falsely reported by the Fake News Liberal Establishment Media™. By the end of the meeting, the secretary had the bear eating out of her hand."

Medvedev agreed that the parties had reached détente. He also insisted, in halting English, that bears present no real danger. "I never visit school but maybe indiscretions in youth with garbage can vandalism and once little playground stalking. This all in past."

The agreement reached by DeVos and Medvedev specifies that there shall be no gunfire so long as no bears join a teachers' union.

ARIZONA APPROVES FIRST AMMO-CENTRIC CHARTER SCHOOL

"Children learn more when the lessons are connected to their daily lives," Mrs. Slaughter told a crowded room of hopeful Scottsdale parents yesterday. She's the mastermind behind Arizona's first ammo-centric charter school. The school's classes will all be built around the children's keen interest in guns and gun-related activities.

She explained the curriculum to the gathered parents. "For math, they'll work with body-count databases. For science, they'll learn how to make gunpowder, and for shop, they'll convert semi-automatics to full autos. For civics, they'll study constitutional law, or at least the Second Amendment. For literature, they'll read a wonderful, modern version of Macbeth. And it's so exciting to think of all the fun they'll have during PE!"

The state's only requirement was that the school be located within 10 miles of the Phoenix Children's Hospital's Pediatric Emergency Department.

"This ain't no dagger which I see before me."

CHILDHOOD OBESITY AND MARKETING

Every 3 years, policymakers and journalists in the United States seem to engage in an orchestrated ritual of hand-wringing upon the release of scores from the Programme for International Student Assessment (PISA) tests. The U.S. scores tend to be rather mediocre, far behind high achievers like Finland. Anyway, in the following piece, I went for the obvious pun.

UNITED STATES TOPS IN PIZZA SCORES

American children maintained their perennial hold on first place in the annual PIZZA competition. The PIZZA (Plump Idle Zesty Ziti Assessment) offers an international report card comparing how well children are doing at becoming lethargic blobs of mush.

Chuck E. Sbarro, the director of PIZZA in the United States, credited a combination of minimal exer-cise, bad diet at home, and vending machines dispensing well-packaged fat and sugar at school. "Ultimately," Sbarro stressed, "the keys to U.S. dominance are our self-destructive habits, constantly reinforced by advertising and marketing in every area of our children's lives."

Although these weighty trends are on track to continue in the United States for the foreseeable future,

Potential Grizzlies, pages 71–72

supremacy in the PIZZA is no longer guaranteed. Many countries are closing the gap. "As junk food purveyors find new markets throughout the world, we will have to work extra hard to maintain our disadvantage," Sbarro advised.

Leaving Japan and Finland in the (Cheeto) dust.

COVID-19

In March of 2020, I started drafting an April Fool's Day newsletter, and I wrote three COVID-19 pieces. As the crisis became more dire, however, I decided it was too painful to laugh. (The policy center did not send off a newsletter on April 1, 2020.) The pain is, of course, still raw. But something else happened: one of the pieces (*Anti-Vaxxers Express Coronavirus Worries*) started to move from parody to reality. The so-called COVIDiot movement took on steam, and the anti-vaccination crowd moved to center stage. I concluded, therefore, that I should offer up these pieces before the craziness of the real world overtakes them.

CORONAVIRUS DECIDES TO GO DIGITAL, FOLLOWING SHIFT TO ONLINE CLASSES

SARS-CoV-2, the coronavirus that causes the COVID-19 disease, is launching an innovative new enterprise in response to changing market conditions. As classes and commercial activity relocate in response to the outbreak, from in-person interactions into virtual space, the virus will expand its own operations from analog to digital.

"Our ancestors could never have conceived of the current technology," explained spokesvirus Cory Pesht. "We need to adapt and follow the

Potential Grizzlies, pages 73–69

customer base. The rest of the world has come so far beyond the days of Typhoid Mary. We can no longer passively wait for the happy coincidence of an asymptomatic carrier with lots of social interactions."

Pesht did not hide his frustration with the inefficiencies of that time-honored process. "Yes, we got lucky this time. But you're not exactly going to conquer the world waiting for generation after generation in those godforsaken bats or civets or pangolins, just hoping for a new host and just the right mutations to break into the big time."

In contrast, widespread opportunities are now available in the computer virus marketplace. In that

"Cory greets 1001110, his digital doppelganger."

crowded arena, SARS-CoV-2 will be competing with a variety of cyber-criminals and mischief-makers, in addition to some bots and state-sponsored efforts. But Pesht is certain that it will be decades before the sphere is completely saturated. "We're confident that there's room for the COVID Digital Initiative, particularly as our users gain ubiquitous access to technology."

Pointing to the current response to the analog coronavirus pandemic, Pesht sees a synergy between the two efforts. "This will be a real nexus of old and new. As the COVID-19 lockdown encourages greater cyber-presence, we see an ever-growing clientele for our digital version."

SCHOOL CLOSINGS FORCES CHANGE IN ICE TACTICS

Agents of the U.S. Immigration and Customs Enforcement (ICE) have been hit hard by the COVID-19 pandemic, as they struggle to cope with the widespread closure of public schools. These schools serve the vital public service of giving ICE agents a convenient way to arrest parents who are in the country without documentation.

Back when schools were serving their proper purpose.

"For the past several years, our agents could simply wait for parents to drop their children off at school," explained Stephen Miller, senior policy advisor to President Trump. "The school closures have placed an enormous new burden on those agents, and at such a difficult time for the president and other real Americans."

Fortunately, $400 million was freed up this spring, when the president decided to end the annual contribution to the World Health Organization. "We hope to divert that funding to ICE," said Miller, "to help offset the added costs they'll have to incur now that those parent-magnets have closed. During a crisis like this, we have to be particularly attentive to ensuring that funding goes to organizations that can do the most good."

ANTI-VAXXERS EXPRESS CORONAVIRUS WORRIES

The anti-vaccine community is keeping a close eye on the devastating COVID-19 pandemic. They are deeply worried that this humanitarian crisis, unprecedented in the modern era, will provoke the development of a new vaccine.

"Right now, we're seeing the honeymoon period before a coronavirus vaccine is developed and before Big Government starts pressuring people

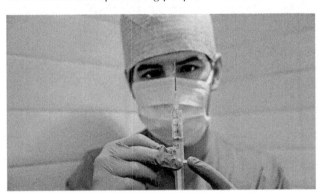

The real threat.

to get vaccinated," declared anti-vaxxer Genevieve Rubella.

The overarching concern voiced by Rubella and her colleagues is that vaccines interfere with the natural process of developing immunities while exposing vaccinated children to aluminum and thimerosal.

"If we accept the large body of research purporting to show vaccines to be safe and effective, we are mere sheep being manipulated by Big Pharma," Rubella explained. "No thank you! I prefer to trust my Facebook friends. That's how I found out that vaccines were invented to sterilize children, depopulate the earth, and slow evolution."

"One friend tweeted me," continued Rubella, "that if our bodies are naturally exposed to coronavirus at the same time that they're exposed to tuberculosis and measles, we might spontaneously evolve into super-beings! We're planning some exposure parties for our families now, ahead of the vaccine outbreak."

Photo Credits

Page xvi Sean Locke Photography/Shutterstock (modified)

Page 2: Pacific Northwest National Laboratory.

Page 4: Steve Bidmead from Pixabay.

Page 9: Peggy und Marco Lachmann-Anke from Pixabay.

Page 10: Sander van der Wel from Netherlands–CC BY-SA.

Page 11: Sandra Gabriel on Unsplash.

Page 12: Neenah History on VisualHunt.com CC BY-NC-SA.

Page 14: Kirk Morales on Unsplash CC0.

Page 16: Global Order of Satan/Wikimedia commons CC BY-SA 4.0

Page 17: Flickr photo from Counse, adapted. Attribution 2.0 Generic.

Page 20: West Side Story (see https://commons.wikimedia.org/wiki/File: George_Chakiris_in_West_Side_Story.jpg)

Page 22: Billion Photos/Shutterstock.

Page 23: Midtown Comics/Wikimedia commons CC0.

Page 26: Pixabay public domain CC0.

Page 27: rawpixel/pixabay.com, with modifications.

Page 28: Tim Ross. CC0 for Public Domain.

Page 29: ccarlstead on Visualhunt.com CC BY-SA.

Potential Grizzlies, pages 77–78
Copyright © 2021 by Information Age Publishing
77

Page 30: Flickr Del Goodchild CC BY-ND 2.0.

Page 31: Pressmaster/Shutterstock.

Page 33: Alexander Raths/Shutterstock.

Page 34: Janko Ferlic from Pexels. Public domain.

Page 36: DeVos: official photo
Shkreli: House Committee on Oversight and Government Reform
Skilling: United States Marshals Service

Page 37: Flikr USFWS Steve Agius.

Page 42: Photo by Håkan Dahlström CC BY 2.0.

Page 43: Spc. Stephanie Cassinos Way (see https://commons.wikimedia
.org/wiki/File:Elementary_school_teaches_more_than_ABCs_
DVIDS218937.jpg).

Page 48:   Gage Skidmore/Flickr, modified.

Page 50: Form PxHere.

Page 51: sirtravelalot/Shutterstock.

Page 54: SpeedKingz/Shutterstock.

Page 56: Kellinahandbasket on Visualhunt.com CC BY 2.0.

Page 57: Ivan_Karpov/Shutterstock.

Page 58: Niklas Gustavsson, Flickr CC BY 2.0.

Page 59: Julia Cameron Pexels.

Page 60: Steve Snodgrass on Visualhunt CC BY 2.0.

Page 64: Public domain.

Page 65: Frankie cordoba on Unsplash.

Page 68: Official White House photo by Shealah Craighead (modiefied).
See https://static.boredpanda.com/blog/wp-content/uploads/
2016/05/adopted-bear-russian-family-stepan-a3.jpg

Page 69: Window & Grove (see https://commons.wikimedia.org/wiki/File:
Ellen_Terry_plays_Lady_Macbeth.jpg), modified.

Page 72: Teguh Mujiono/Shutterstock.

Page 74: Peggy und Marco Lachmann-Anke from Pixabay.

Page 75: Wikicommons, https://commons.wikimedia.org/wiki/File:US_
Immigration_and_Customs_Enforcement_arrest.jpg

Page 76: Dimitri-houtteman-qBhpPxW3ESs-unsplash.

Made in the USA
Columbia, SC
17 December 2020